Modern Curriculum Press
**BEGINNING
TO
READ**
Series

IASA/ESEA Title **1**
Nonpublic School **Program**

GEORGE WASHINGTON

ISBN 0-8136-5963-9 (paperback)

4 5 6 7 8 9 10   02 01 00 99 98

George
Washington

by Clara Ingram Judson

Illustrated by Bob Patterson

MODERN CURRICULUM PRESS
Cleveland • Toronto

When George Washington was a boy, he lived on a farm in Virginia. His father had pigs and cows, geese and chickens. He had horses too.

George liked the horses best. He had his own pony, Whitefoot.

George was always a good rider. He liked to ride his pony over the fields.

Some days he rode Whitefoot to school.
The school was in a little cabin on the farm.

Later George went to a better school.
There he learned more about writing and
arithmetic.

But George Washington did not go
to school very much. He learned about
horses and farming from his father and his
brothers.

He learned good manners from watching
people.

When George was eleven years old, his father died. After that George often stayed at Mount Vernon, the home of his brother Lawrence.

George liked Lawrence's home. There were always parties and friends at Mount Vernon.

George was a tall, strong, good-looking boy. Lawrence's friends liked George. They treated him like a man.

One day when George was at his mother's
home, he found some tools and a long chain.

"Those are your father's surveying tools,"
his mother said. "Your father was a surveyor."

"What is a surveyor?" George asked.

"He is a man who measures land. When
people buy farms, the land must be surveyed so
they will know where the farm begins and ends."

Maybe I can be a surveyor, George thought.

When he was nearly fifteen, George went
to see a surveyor in town.

"I would like to be a surveyor, sir,"
he said. "Will you teach me?"

"It is hard work," the man said. "I walk
for miles and work in the rain and cold and mud."

"I could carry your tools, sir," George said.
"And I can make maps."

"Come in," the surveyor said. He needed
a boy who could make maps.

So George began to learn to be a surveyor.

When George was sixteen years old, he went on a long trip with a surveying party. They had to measure wilderness land that belonged to one of Lawrence's friends.

On that trip George learned about living in the wilderness. He slept in a tent or under the stars. He shot wild turkeys and cooked the meat over a fire.

The surveying party often saw trappers and traders. One night an Indian war party camped near the surveyors.

George had a little book. In it he wrote down what he saw on the trip. He wrote about the Indians' war dance:

"They clear a large circle and make a great fire in the middle. Then they sit around it. A speaker tells them how they are to dance. The best dancer jumps up and runs and jumps about the ring. The rest then begin..."

In the next year George learned more
about surveying. When he was not working,
he often stayed at the home of a cousin.

George had a good time hunting and
playing games with his cousins. Everyone
liked George, and they liked to hear about
his trips.

One day when George was at Mount Vernon, Lawrence said to him:

"I hear that a surveyor is needed in the next county. You must pass a test to get the job. I think you can pass it."

George rode a long way to take that test. He passed it and got the job.

He was just seventeen years old. He had a man's job. Lawrence was proud of his brother.

George was now over six feet tall and very big and strong. No one could ride a horse better than he could. Men liked him and trusted him. He was a born leader.

As he did his surveying, George learned more and more about his country, its big rivers and rich lands. He learned to love it more and more. He thought he would like to serve his country.

When he was twenty-one years old, George Washington became a major in the Virginia army.

He was still a surveyor too and still took long trips into the wilderness.

Some nights he stayed at places where traders and trappers were staying. Often they talked as they sat around the fire.

One night a trader said, "I hear the French are coming down from Canada."

"Yes," a trapper said. "The Indians are with them. They're building a fort way up near Lake Erie."

George had heard about the fort from other traders. He knew it would mean trouble between England and France.

At that time, Virginia and the other American colonies belonged to England. The English king sent a governor to rule each of his colonies.

In Europe, England and France were nearly always at war. Both countries claimed land in America.

Then George heard that the king had ordered the governor of Virginia to tell the French to get out. But who would take the message?

The French fort near Lake Erie was very far away. George had never gone so far. But he liked adventure, and he wanted to serve his country.

George went to the governor of Virginia.

He said, "I will take your message to the French."

Some other men and an Indian guide went with George. The trip was long and very hard. It was in winter, and very cold. But they got to the French fort.

When he got back to Virginia, George said to the governor, "The French will not go. They mean to build more forts. They are making friends of the Indians."

"We will make them go," said the governor.

Soon after that, war began. Soldiers from England and from the colonies fought to drive out the French and Indians.

After seven years the war was over. The English won. They kept all their American colonies and took Canada from the French.

When the war was over, George Washington was a colonel. He had led the soldiers of the Virginia colony.

Now he could stop being a soldier. He could go back to Mount Vernon. Lawrence had died, and Mount Vernon belonged to George.

George added new rooms to the house and sent to England for new furnishings.

Then he married Martha Custis.

A busy, happy time now began for George Washington. Day after day he rode out over his farms. He made plans for plowing, planting, and harvesting.

He liked to try new ways of farming,
and he planted new kinds of crops. He
sold the crops and saw that they were shipped.
He wrote about all of this in a book.

Besides looking after the farms,
Washington had to look after his people.
They lived on his farms and worked for him.

Washington still served Virginia too.
He helped to make the laws for the colony.

As time went on, trouble began between the American colonies and England.

More and more, people in the colonies felt they were Americans, not Englishmen.

"We want to buy and sell goods wherever we can, not just in England," they said.

"We do not want to be taxed by England. We want to make our own laws."

Some of the Americans would not obey the English laws.

The English king sent soldiers to make the Americans obey his laws.

Many people in Virginia and the other colonies wanted to be free of England.

Americans knew that if they wanted their freedom, they must fight for it. So war began with England.

America needed a general to lead the army.

Men said, "We need a leader who is brave and wise. We need a leader who can train an army.

We need a man who will never give up until freedom is won."

They chose George Washington.

Washington wanted to do all he could for his country.

He was not sure he was the best leader for the army. But when they chose him, he said:

"I will do my best."

The American soldiers were proud of
their general.

"He looks like a general," they said.
"And he knows how to fight."

Washington worked to make an army out
of the farm boys. He had to train the men.
He had to work very hard to get food and
clothing and guns for them.

During one winter at Valley Forge, the
soldiers were sick and hungry. Many of
them had no shoes.

The American soldiers won some battles, but they lost many more than they won. Still Washington never gave up. After eight long, hard years, the war for freedom was won.

General Washington was very happy that he could go back to Mount Vernon. But soon his country called him to serve again. He was elected the first president of the United States of America.

His trip to New York City to take the office of president was like a long, long parade. At every town people waved flags and cheered for George Washington.

They threw flowers before his horse's feet.

Being the first president of the United States was a very hard job. It was not only a new country, but it had a new kind of government—government not by a king, but by the people. Would this new kind of government work?

Just as he led the army in the long,
hard years of the war, Washington now worked
to build the new country. He made the new
government work, and he made the country strong.

After eight years as president, he went
back to Mount Vernon. How happy he was to
be just Farmer Washington again!

For three more years he enjoyed his life as a farmer and planter.

When he died, the whole country was sad. One man said what the people of America thought of George Washington:

"First in war, first in peace, and first in the hearts of his countrymen."

GEORGE WASHINGTON

Reading Level: Level Three. *George Washington* has a total vocabulary of 378 words. It has been tested in third grade classes, where it was read with ease.

Uses of This Book: An excellent introduction to history. Through this biography of our first president, children in the primary grades will gain an appreciation of why we honor George Washington as the "father of his country."

Word List

5 when
George('s)
Washington
was
a
boy(s)
he
lived(ing)
on
farm(s)(ing)(er)
in
Virginia
his
father('s)
had
pigs
and
cows
geese
chickens
horse(s)('s)
too
like(d)
the
best
own
pony
Whitefoot
always
good(s)
ride(r)

to
over
fields
6 some
day(s)
rode
school
little
cabin
later
went
better
there
learn(ed)
more
about
writing
arithmetic
but
did
not
go
very
much
from
brother(s)
manners
watching
people
7 eleven
year(s)

old
died
after
that
often
stay(ed)(ing)
at
Mount
Vernon
home
of
Lawrence('s)
were
parties
friend(s)
tall
strong
good-looking
they
treated
him
man('s)
8 one
mother('s)
found
tools
long
chain
those
are
your

survey(ing)(ed)
said
surveyor(s)
what
is
asked
who
measure(s)
land(s)
buy
must
be
so
will
know(s)
where
begin(s)
ends
maybe
I
can
thought
near(ly)
fifteen
see
would
town
sir
you
teach
me

hard
work(ing)(ed)
walk
for
miles
rain
cold
mud
could
carry
make
maps
come
need(ed)
began
10 sixteen
trip(s)
with
party
wilderness
belonged
slept
tent
or
under
stars
shot
wild
turkeys
cooked
meat

fire
saw
trapper(s)
trader(s)
night(s)
an
Indian(s)(s')
war
camped
book
it
wrote
down
dance(r)
clear
large
circle
great
middle
then
sit
around
speaker
tell(s)
them
how
jumps
up
runs
ring
rest
12 next
cousin(s)
time
hunting
playing
games
everyone
hear
13 county
pass(ed)
test
get
job
way(s)

take
got
just
seventeen
proud
now
six
feet
big
no
than
men
trusted
born
lead(er)
14 as
country
its
rivers
rich
love
serve(d)
twenty-one
became
major
army
15 still
took
into
places
talked
sat
French
coming
Canada
yes
they're
build(ing)
fort(s)
Lake
Erie
16 heard
other
knew

mean
trouble
between
England
France
American(s)
colonies
English
king
sent
governor
rule
each
Europe
both
countries
claimed
America
order(ed)
out
message
far
away
never
gone
adventure
want(ed)
17 guide
winter
18 back
making
soon
soldier(s)
fought
drive
seven
won
all
their
colonel
led
colony
stop
being

19 added
new
rooms
house
furnishings
married
Martha
Custis
busy
happy
made
plans
plowing
plant(ing)(ed)(er)
harvesting
20 try
kind(s)
crops
sold
shipped
this
besides
look(ing)(s)
helped
laws
21 felt
Englishmen
we
sell
wherever
do
taxed
by
our
obey
22 many
free
if
freedom
fight
general
brave
wise
train
give

until
chose
sure
my
24 food
clothing
guns
during
Valley
Forge
sick
hungry
shoes
25 battles
lost
gave
eight
called
again
elected
first
president
United
States
26 New York
City
office
parade
every
waved
flags
cheered
threw
flowers
before
27 only
government
29 three
enjoyed
life
whole
sad
peace
hearts
countrymen